LOVE IS HAPPINESS:

Destined to be together

By

Nancy W. Robinson

ACKNOWLEDGEMENT

To Kingston who inspired me to tell our story when we never knew we had one. And the support of my siblings, Mira and david. Who has been my pillar of support throughout.

Thanks for the love and understanding.

TABLE OF CONTENT

- Chapter 1:Love at first sight
- Chapter 2:Relationship and friends
- Chapter 3:Disappointment
- Chapter 4:Deeply in love
- Chapter 5:My first kiss
- Chapter 6:Heartbroken
- Chapter 7:Family issues
- Chapter 8:Keeping love alive
- Chapter 9:Promotion
- Chapter 10:Wishing me happy birthday
- Chapter 11:Separated from my love
- Chapter 12:Happily married ever
- Dedication and conclusion

Chapter 1

I was in the church, waiting patiently for the service to come to an end, eager to go home.

A young handsome guy came inside, seeing him at the first sight makes my heart beat in a way I have never experienced before. This kind of feeling has never happened to me.

I was silent for a few minutes, and happy. I stopped for a while to listen to my heartbeat, I felt so emotional. What is this? I asked myself but no response, is this love and why am I feeling this way, I said to myself.

Am too young to fall in love, moreover, I am just 14 years old, I told myself. Finally, the program came to an end." HAPPY SUNDAY", greeted one of my friends, after the program, the man of God(pastor), which was my dad, asked the choir to welcome the "first-time comer" with a nice song. As a chorister, I stood up while the others joined me in welcoming the first-time comer with a melody song.

Still thinking about that gentle guy, asking myself a lot of questions, I don't know who to talk to about how I am feeling. Who is this guy, and where does he live? I went into my room. Then I stopped for a while to listen. My plan was not to eavesdrop, but there was something about the conversation that made it interesting.

My junior brother, who was 12 years old, appears to be the narrator. He was telling my other little sister, who was our last born. Discussing the handsome guy, who came to our church. The guy is so talented, he knows a lot about instruments, especially in the church. He loves everything that has to do with instruments in church, and lastly, he's cheerful.

I found myself laughing silently before I let myself go into the room. They were used to my unannounced bargaining because I am their senior sister, they have no right to question me. They learn to respect my opinion.

My mother, who people refer to as mummy G.O, was loved by everyone, she's a gentle woman who loves everyone accordingly irrespective of your tribe or status. There was a great affinity between my mum and me. I expressed most of my feelings to her because of her maturity. I love her so much with so much respect.

It was so bright in the morning.

Sophia, who was our last born rushed her food, stood up to pack her books, preparing to go to school. She was astonished to see her brother William slowly eating his meal, undisturbed by any sound.

"William, aren't you going to school? She said,

What's your business Sophia, you are on your way to school already, so go to your school hypocrite. William has no zeal, shifting his gaze back to his food unconcerned. In a few minutes, Sophia had gone to school.

I was in my room dressing up, looking so beautiful. Yeah I know you are surprised by that word, I took after my mom. I know I am beautiful, but at the same time, I am having cold feet. I was scared thinking about what my school result will be, what if I fail I won't get admitted to grade 10.

My dad noticed my reaction and asked me "why are you scared" didn't you perform well in your examination? He said I didn't give him any reply.

Finally, we were at the school gate, straight up to the principal's office, waiting for the arrival of my principal. Not quite long after he came in, with some introduction and payment, my result was handed over to me. Seeing it made me smile. I went to fill out some forms at the head office, to process my admission, and finally, I was admitted to my dream department as a medical student.

Finally, it was a dream coming true, I was happy. The news came as a pleasant surprise to my mom and my siblings, they were happy for me.

Within two days the tailor I gave my dress to, called me to collect my dress, so happy. Little by little my dream is coming true not knowing I just started the race, I never knew it's gonna be a difficult task for me, thinking everything in this world is easy but as a child, I didn't realize that the word itself is a race.

"Life has been a race from one generation to another with only a few people getting to fulfill their dream. Many keep running just to have the basic things of life. They have no clue about where they are headed. They end up getting nowhere because they are running aimlessly. such people lack self-esteem," my mother said, looking straight into my eyes, I was confused. Life, therefore, is about learning to understand how to face and overcome challenges.

My first day at school was very interesting, I mingle with a lot of people. Am Jovial and cheerful, I mingle with people around me as a family. I was calm, I have no best friend but with time I keep on associating with people"vice-versa". After some weeks I got in touch with a girl, short and chocolate, we became best friends although I met some of my old friends that we both went to the same school, and most especially my "boyfriend".

Boyfriend indeed, people call him my boyfriend because of the strong affinity between us. He has been my favorite friend since childhood. I feel happy when people call him my boyfriend. At times I blush. With time I fell in love with him but I was too shy to confess my true feelings to him. I care so much about him, and I try my best to satisfy him, yet I didn't tell him about my secret feelings.

David is a guy who loves girls a lot, but still, I didn't give up on him. But on a faithful day like this popped up, I was angry that I couldn't take it again, I was reprimanding him about his character, fleeting with girls all around, but to my greatest surprise, he shouted at me.

David POV

"After all you are just a friend to me nothing more, so how dare you tell me what to do or not, it's high time you know your limit, you are not my time, and don't think I'll fall in love with you".

Hearing this makes my heart chartered like broken glass, so short of words. Someone who I deeply love with all my heart could break my heart, I could not believe my ears." Sobering all day long reminded me of the sweet memories we spent together. Whenever I feel cold he'll always sit beside me to cuddle me, I remember those days, I wept.

With time I learned to move on and forget about everything that happened, since then I decided not to fall in love again, the only thing left in me was hatred.

But it was something different from what I felt the other day I was in church. I could not believe I could ever fall in love with any other guy after the incident that transpired between David and me.

The love I have this time was stronger than that of David. I didn't allow it to affect my education. Months passed by likewise weeks and everything was going smoothly.

I know you'll be asking about David or his whereabouts, or what happened after. After the incident, I apologized to him for my rude action and he did the same but the feelings were gone. The friendship between us was intact but not like before, but after some months he left the school and relocated to another city. Since then we parted ways. I missed him so much not because I still have feelings for him but because he was my best friend, that was how our friendship ended.

Chapter 2

"Preparing to go to school"
I paused outside the door.
"Mummy, I shouted.
Yes, Emily, what is it?
Please add some tokens to my money, I said. Okay, I'll do that Emily, she said.
Thank you, mummy, I exited the room.
On my way to school, after a few steps, I saw this gentle guy I met in church the other day, outside his house brushing without putting on a Singlet. His chest was something else, I was amazed, staring at that broad chest and his eight packs, his arms, and his abs. "Wow what an amazing guy". I was blushing until both faces came in contact, I shifted my gaze and pretended as if I was looking somewhere else.

To my greatest surprise after a few steps forward I looked back again to take a few glances at the mysterious guy but to my surprise, he was staring at me and we both smiled. On my way to school, I was thinking about the guy, his face, his smile, his chest, and everything. I wasn't thinking about my life anymore. Instead I was daydreaming about him, I lose total control of myself, to sleep at night became difficult. Each time I closed my eyes all I could see was his face.

A few weeks later, we became friends, and by introducing himself as "Henry", to the choir. We welcomed him to our midst, I was really happy thinking it was an opportunity to get closer to him. Finally, we became friends. Henry is such a gentle and caring guy, this was my first time falling in love with someone I don't know, "love at first sight".

I wake up so early in the morning to do all my chores as quickly as possible just to see his face before going to school. This love is something else "smiling". Hardly did I know this is just the beginning. Henry's case was different, a guy I don't know became someone closer to my heart.
My mother, a caring woman full of wisdom, would sometimes sit me down to advise me.
"Emily you're still a child, but there are certain things you need to know about life, marriage, and sex. Marriage is bound to happiness if there's adequate planning before and after the celebration. But nowadays most of our youth are not patient, they sell their body to a guy just to prove how much they love him. It's so unfortunate that most girls who aren't ready for marriage engage in sex just to appeal to their boyfriend, during this process, some get unwanted pregnancies which will eventually bring shame to their families. My daughter, I plead with you, as you are aware that you are the firstborn and also a daughter of a pastor, always remember the child of who you are*, after the word of advice she pats me on my shoulder.
Mom, I'll never disappoint you, or bring shame to our family. I promised her.

After the discussion, I thought deeply about it. For my dream to come to pass I have to leave and forget all irrelevant stuff. On that day I promise my mom I'll work harder and fulfill all her wishes. Still, I didn't forget about Henry. "Smile" yes he's mine I said.

A month after,The friendship between Henry and I got stronger, I made use of his notes to read ahead of topics in class, since we are from the same department, but he's done, through that we started communicating very well which makes the bond stronger.

As usual, I went to lend them one of his textbooks, and he gave it to me with a smile. I went through the textbook and jotted down some useful points I needed.

A few hours later.

After some hours, I decided to return the textbook, then I felt something within me, I couldn't understand myself, my feelings were getting the better of me, I summoned the courage to tell him how I felt. I was scared to confront him, but still, I don't want to lose another opportunity of getting what I want just like in the case of "David".
I had no choice but to reveal my true feelings to Henry.

I make use of the note I borrowed from him to send a message to him. At the front of the book cover I wrote down my feelings. I LOVE YOU.
"My heart gradually responds, gradually revives, gradually relieved". I returned the book to him as it was very late, he could not see what I wrote, but I know the next day he will see it. Thanks for the book Henry, I said. He bid me farewell, I exited his house and headed to my place.
I was happy throughout the night. I was able to pour out my mind, and I was at ease as if a burden had been carried away from my head. The joy in me that night is something I can't explain.

Next day
I was in the church all alone reading some scripture, the fact is my house and church were in the same compound so whenever I feel bored at home I do come to church to sit down, at times I sing and at times I read novels or scripture. I was in the church around that afternoon time all alone at home. Then I heard some footsteps, lifting my eyes to see who it was, fortunately, it was Henry (my crush).

Henry
Good afternoon Emily, and how are you doing, he said.
I'm fine Henry and what about.
Same here Emily.
Wow what are you doing here Henry, I said.
Hope no problem.
Not at all Emily, I'm fine dear.
I could not believe my ears, Henry refers to me as "dear". My heart trembles seeing him walking up to me.
I saw your message Emily, I paused a little bit, I was nervous, it was as if my blood was dripping out of my body.
After some silence, "I let the cat out of the bag". Yes, Henry, everything I said was the truth, I said. He made a slight smirk, Emily. I love your confidence, you are such a beautiful girl and you're smart as well, don't worry I'll think about it and get back to you. I was so happy about his response, it felt as if I should give him a tight hug.
Alright thanks, Henry, I said and he left.

My heart was filled with joy throughout the night, it was also my first time asking a guy out or saying out my feelings.

Chapter 3

Good evening, Henry, we both exchanged greetings. Am so glad you honor my calling and you came Emily, it's not Henry I said. He offered me a seat, and I sat beside him and narrated how I felt. He was happy about it. I was also happy seeing him smiling, as a lady all I was expecting was "YES". he called my name, Emily I love you so much but just as a friend, it is so unfortunate Emily, I have a girlfriend friend already, do I can't accept you as my bae, am sorry Emily.

Hearing those words, I felt disappointed, my heart aches a lot. All I could do was hold back my tears. I wasn't myself anymore, sobered. "Sometimes we create our heartbreak through expectation. I was expecting a positive answer from him but unfortunately, he has a life partner already. "Life isn't measured by the number of breaths we take, but by the moment that takes our breath away".

Sometimes when we get disappointed, it makes us stronger, one's best success comes after their greatest disappointment.

I'll never give up, the fall of a man isn't the end of a man. I'll keep on striving until I get what I want. I wasn't obsessed but it was true love, a genuine one. I reasoned with what he said, then I decided to make him my best buddy. "I know some will say am foolish", but that's not the case. Love isn't selfish, just because of your happiness you don't need to ruin someone else's own. When it comes to love, it requires sacrifice.

Time flew very fast, we became tight friends which was placed on trust and sincerity. Our parents were having strange feelings but the real fact is we are just best friends nothing more. His problem became my problem, and vice versa. We enjoyed each other's company and were ready to face every challenge that comes our way.

Ummm.... For almost three months, we've been together as a good friend, it got to an extent that our friendship became strong that no argument could break. People started gossiping around, and some were jealous.

We were having some special program at church, and during the program, I noticed Henry was somehow dull till the end of the program. After the program I went to meet him, dude why are you so dull today? What's wrong my dear? What on earth could have happened that makes you unhappy?

I offer him a cup of water to calm him down. He called out my name, Emily with a shaky voice, he was crying.

Henry what happened, I was so scared seeing him crying, tell me what is wrong Henry, you are scaring me, why aren't you saying anything, I was scared.

Am heartbroken Emily. My girlfriend cheated on me, she left me to be with my friend. Hearing those words, I pitied him. I was so sad for him.

How did it happen Henry and how did you find out about it?

He narrates everything to me and how it all happened, at that moment I don't know if I should be happy or sympathize with him. But as a human being who has feelings, I consoled him while he rested his head on my lap. I felt so bad for him because I know how it feels, having gone through that before, in the case of David, it was just that we weren't dating then but still similar to Henry's case. Take heart Henry, I know how it feels when your loved ones disappoint you.

I encourage him to stay happy and move on. "Be thankful for what you have Henry and you'll end up having more, but if you concentrate on what you lose, you'll never have enough". He smiled a little bit. I was happy to see him smiling. Never let a bad situation bring out the worst in you, choose to stay positive and be strong for my sake Henry.

I escort him back to his house to make sure he gets home safely, such people can't be left alone because of the depression. On our way going, I cracked an expensive joke.

"Henry, don't worry, they are beautiful girls out there, you'll see better ones, forget about her, she's your ex already and if you want you can come for me, I'm here for you. Stop that Emily, he burst into laughter and we both smiled, take care of yourself Henry, goodnight dear bye, I exited his place.

I never knew that joke would become reality. That night was another love story entirely and a new beginning for both of us,huh.

Love is just a feeling you can never get rid of so easily, I was able to sleep comfortably that night.

A few days later.

On my way out I jumped into him, both shocked and we burst into laughter. Where are you heading to, we said at the same time. "Smile"

I'm on my way to work Emily, Henry, are you sure you are going to work? Yes, I am Emily, okay oh, wish you all the best dude.

Thanks, Emily, we both laughed and parted ways.

Still expecting one day he will accept me and fill my life with so much love.

"When there's life there is hope. hope is not meant for those who are dead, although it may tarry never lose hope on that thing you want, keep on striving soon or later you'll get the best results.

I didn't give up nor did I allow my education to be affected in any way because of my love story.

Two months later

As usual, I woke up so early, preparing to go to school, I did all my chores as fast as possible, to get to school on time.

On my way there, I met Henry outside his house waiting to bid me farewell.

Hi, Emily.

Good morning Henry, how are you doing, how was your night dear?

It was great Emily.

Okay dear, I am off to school. See you later.

Bye!!!!

On my way there, I felt someone was trying to reach out to me, I ignored that, thinking it was just an imagination. I moved forward, but later on, I checked my back just to confirm if someone is calling out to me. To my surprise, I saw my junior brother waving at me, breathing heavily due to the energy he lost while running.

I stopped to wait for him, why are running?

Hope no problem, no my sister.
Henry said I should give you this envelope.
Envelope, I was surprised, for what?
I don't know my sister. Okay, thank you. I'll read that later and give it to me.
I was troubled, what could be inside this envelope? I was eager to know what was written inside it. I could not check it, I was late for school already. I had to work fast to get to school as quickly as possible. Unfortunately, the assembly was over already, and when I got to the school entrance, I headed up to my class.
I was staring at the envelope, there was no free time for us during the entire day. I kept the letter in a safe place so no one would see it. Impatient is about to kill me (smiling).
The school was fun. School life is the best.

Chapter 4

So late in the night, I decided to check what was in the letter. to my greatest surprise, it was a proposal letter. Wow, I shouted while blushing.
"Dear Emily, I appreciate your effort and patience. Even though I never consider you as my girlfriend, still you never give up, you've always loved me so much. Now is the right time to consider you as my life partner, you are so unique and special. You are amazing and lovely, your dark eyes are so charming and your complexity, I wander so much not knowing my true love is by my side. You are the one I want to find to tell that I need you all my life, from this day on till the rest of my life. Only4me, you're the only thing I want to see forever in my eyes, in my world, and in everything I do. Your sight is the only sight that will ever bring me peace. I wouldn't promise you heaven and earth, but I have the only thing precious to me to give you. And that is my heart. "will you accept my heart of love as your boyfriend and life partner".
If I could give you any gift, I'd give you love and laughter, and a peaceful heart. a special dream and Joy Forever after. let me do so please!!!, I will be the best you can find. Please accept me Emily and I promise to make you happy for the rest of your life.
" I love you so much" Only4me. My eyes were full of tears of joy, and my heart was beating so heavily, at last, victory is mine, Henry is mine... I was lost in joy... I wept. I couldn't sleep that night, it was one of the longest nights I had, due to how happy I was. I'm glad that he's my boyfriend. I can't imagine anyone else taking his place if I hadn't got the opportunity to tell him my feelings then he would've still been my best friend instead of my boyfriend.
I dialed Henry's number. I wanted him to assure me that what he wrote in that letter is true. I wanted him to tell me that he will fulfill his promise. I wanted him to tell me that he will keep his word no matter what. I just needed to be assured.
"Hi Henry, I said.
" Henry, I saw your message through the letter you sent to me, I asked, fear and happiness talking over me.
"Yeah, I sent the letter. you sound somehow. Is everything okay? He asked me.
can we see tomorrow, I said.
" Emily, don't worry, I know what you want to say. I won't hurt you, "he said and I believe him. That is all I needed to hear. I was able to sleep well last night.
I knew that Henry meant every word he said, I could trust him.

Next day
Emily good morning, where are you?
"Yeah, I'm almost there, Henry.
He came to pick me up, let's go, he said. I nodded and followed him. It was a restaurant not that far from our place.
"What do you want to eat or drink Emily?
I'm okay for now, I was blushing so I decided to look at the floor so that my blush could vanish from my cheek. Lol
When he finished talking, silence fell in the restaurant, no one spoke. There's a feeling of happiness inside my heart knowing that he loves me so much.
" Emily I love you so much", he said, out of the blue. Are you serious about that Henry?

Yes, I am in love with you although I don't know when I had these feelings for you all I could remember is I love you so much I can't live without you, I know I might have hurt your feelings before but please accept me I am in love with you Emily.
Emily I can't imagine living my life without you by my side, it is true I didn't respond to your love, I made you wait. I'm sorry for causing you so much pain Emily. Please accept me into your life, he said.
I don't want anyone to come in between us especially now that I have fallen for you.
After a pause, he said, I want you to be my soulmate forever.
It seems unbelievable but the look on his face told me that he was telling me the truth. hearing him say that I'm his love makes me smile.
Henry, I've always loved you right from the beginning even Up to Now I'm Still in Love With You, This is my happiest moment ever Henry.
Henry, I accept you to be my life partner From this day on till eternity.
He smiled and said thank you so much, he gave me a tight hug and pecked me on the cheek, and looked at his wristwatch. It's late already Emily, let's go home.
That was the beginning of our love story. Getting home I saw my mom on the veranda. I knew that would be another question waiting to hit me.
" Where are you coming from She asked me. I don't know what to say. I'm confused.
"Mu.....my, I'm coming from Henry's place, I took one of my assignments to him, I said. "Oh You should have told me already, am sorry mom, No problem Go inside and have your dinner, my dear. Instantly I went inside after the movie and dinner I went straight to my room to sleep.
Henry was in my room
"Here is the blanket, " he said while handing the blanket to me.
Thanks, I said, I took the blanket from him, my finger brushed with his own and I felt a spark as if I was electrocuted. I don't know what happened to me next, I started leaning on him and I hugged him tightly. I don't know how the courage to hug him came inside of me.
for a few minutes, we were like this. I love this position. I moved closer to the warmth of his body. He smelled so good. very intoxicating. Then I kissed him on his lips.
" For every action, there is always an equal reaction. To my surprise, Henry gave the opposite reaction, which was his hand on my waist.
Our bodies were touching each other. I could feel the vibes. We started kissing romantically and moaning in pleasure.
" Emily, what are you doing? I could sense the shock in the voice.
My eyes opened suddenly, I was wide awake now. I sat on my bed realizing it was a dream
O. M. G, I was sweating. my emotions are getting over me, I said.
I rose from the bed and went straight to the kitchen. I was feeling thirsty, luckily I found a glass of water, and I filled my stomach. Am intoxicated by this love.

Chapter 5

It was around 1:00 p.m. I was sitting on the sofa busy reading some romantic novel.

Since it was Saturday I had no work to do, I decided to keep myself busy by reading my best book(how to communicate with strangers).

Suddenly, There was a knock on our door. " Who could it be? The door was opened, and to my greatest surprise, it was Henry. He was putting on a white top and blue joggers. How can a person look so damn cute?

" I decided to check on you since I was bored so I came by. What are you busy doing all alone inside Emily?

" I'm bored also, so I decided to read some novels. He smiled at me. Why are you laughing, I asked him.

"Oh, it's nothing, Emily.

Alright sit down, then we were quiet.

" Do you miss me, Emily? I wasn't prepared to answer this question so I just asked him, why are you asking?

"Hum... Nothing"

I didn't miss you, I said. He still had a smile on his face. Emily, you should know one thing: You don't know how to lie. I know you are missing me, just spill that out, my love. His words make me smile. We spent the whole day playing games, Chatting, and dancing. I love you so much Emily, he said And kissed me on the forehead.

My heart beats faster. I put my hand on my chest trying to calm myself down. I got up from the sofa, blushing.

It's late already. Let me be on my way.

" Alright Henry. He looked so hot and sexy I said to myself !!!!

I decided to escort him to the gate after everything. We exited the sitting room. I was about to go when he held my hand, I could sense some sparks and my heart pounder. I love the position. This is the first time that Henry romantically holds my hand. I'm having great difficulty hiding my excitement at seeing him holding my hands. I gave him a tight hug and left. That day was so memorable I couldn't retain that joy in me. I never thought that my crush or should I say my boyfriend could be so romantic, For which I was grateful. I went back to my room. Gosh, my emotions are getting the better of me.

So late at night, I was trying to find some solutions to my assignment. By now I should have gotten it but it was taking so much of my time. Becoming a doctor is not easy it will be hard but it isn't impossible.

Emily, You've been working day and night without eating properly, it's affecting your health, she said.

Mom, I don't care about my health. I just want to fulfill my dream, I said to her, my eyes still glued to my book and laptop. Okay, my daughter, I understand. But you need the energy to work on getting your goals, She said to me.

She was right. I won't be able to read more if I'm weak. I need to be strong, I need more energy to be ready. Seeing the expression on my face. My mom smiled at me and offered me sliced bread with butter. Thank you mom, my mouth was still stuffed with bread. she laughed at me, you are so naughty Emily, she smiled. I love it whenever my mom smiles.

Good morning Emily and I said in unison. " How are things going in the house? " He asked next.
" Everything is fine Henry.
" How was your night?" I asked him.
It was pleasant my baby, I missed you so much, dear baby girl.
"Awnnn That's so nice of you"
Can we see today if you don't mind dear, Oh no problem dear, I'm available in the afternoon, I said.
Okay dear, I should go now, stay safe Emily.
"You too, I said.
" Bye"
" Bye"
I ended the call.
For a few minutes, I was confused and didn't know where to start with my house chores. After a while, I decided to arrange the house and look at some of my clothes. A few hours later, I was done with that.

" what should I wear? I was standing in front of the wardrobe, selecting an outfit to put on, so Henry would love me the most. Finally, I got a short armless gown looking so pretty in that gown. After a while, Henry called me and asked.
" where are you?
Am at home dear, well prepared. Okay, I'm on my way, he hung up. for a few minutes, I was waiting for him.
An hour later.....
My phone started ringing. I looked at the caller ID Henry was calling.
" Hello, "I said on the phone.
"Emily, I'm around already, I'm standing in front of your door.
Indeed, Henry was standing there, holding his phone close to his ear. He was waving at me with a smile on his cute face. He laughed and I smiled.
" You look even more beautiful when you blush. I love to see you blushing. hearing this made me blush even more.
``What would you like to eat Henry, "I told him, trying to avoid it so that he could stop saying things that would make me blush.
He laughed, I know what you're trying to do, he said. as he gave me a cute smile.
We were sitting on the bed eating our meal while watching a movie.
" Emily, don't worry I will keep you entertained," he said and winked at me. I was surprised that my boyfriend just winked at me.
"Emily, can we make out? He suggested.
I was short of words, when did he become so forward all of a sudden?
I could not think of anything to say at that moment. " You are kidding me aren't you? He looked a little bit amazed by my question. He leaned forward while I did the same and our lips met. He kissed me. I hope I am not daydreaming again. I asked myself by pinching myself, then I realized it was the real fact. Henry kissed me.

I was blushing and a little bit shy. I took my face away to avoid him staring at me, but instead, he came closer to me, and he held onto my waist. I was craving more of it but I decided not to allow my emotions to get in the way.
He leaned again and started kissing me. I never thought that anybody could be this gentle while kissing. Bringing me closer to him. I could feel the warmth of his body. We continued to kiss for a few minutes, our bodies were even closer, I never thought that I would be in such a position with Henry. I never thought that I would make out with him. Henry kisses me again and again. He's such an amazing kisser. It feels so good. **" indeed it was my first kiss".**

Chapter 6

Mummy

" Yes Emily, what is it?

"I want to go out with one of my friends today".

Can I mom?

Oh no problem Emily, make sure you come home on time. Okay, Mom, I gave her a tight hug.

Truly I wasn't going out to see my friends, but to see Henry.

My mum trusts me so much that she had no opposition about where I'm going.

I sat on my bed smiling to myself remembering what transpired between Henry and me. I was daydreaming with my hair looking like a bird's nest. It's just so lovely, my First Kiss was so memorable and something I can't forget.

" By this time I was done cleaning the house and preparing to eat, there was a very joyous atmosphere in the air because of my new promotion, everybody in the house was happy. Finally, I'm in second grade. Until now Henry did not know about my promotion. I was busy at home due to the joyous atmosphere in the house. The experience was thrilling. I picked up my phone to call Henry to inform him that I won't be able to meet up with him today.

" Hello my love, " I said.

" How are you, baby girl?

I'm fine dear and you.

All is well Emily, are you still coming dear, he asked.

No, my love, I can't come over, moreover, I have good news for you, I'm sure by the time you hear it you'll be happy for me.

"Hey Emily, don't keep me in suspense.

Wow, you look so cute whenever you are a little bit nervous, I said, pulling his legs with a smile on my face.

Henry you won't believe it, have arrived already, your baby is now a big girl.

Have been promoted to grade 11, Henry.

" wow is shouted exclaimed"

Wow, I'm so happy for you Emily, finally, my baby is now a big girl, he said. Hey, dude stop making me blush, anyway thanks so much, I said.

Now I see the reason why you said you're not coming to my place, Emily.

Yes my love my parents won't allow me to leave because of my achievement, they are so excited.

" Oh I understand Emily, don't bother yourself, don't worry when next we see I'm going to celebrate it for you, I'm so proud of you for making it.

I shouted, will you do that for me? If you're trying to tease me you better stop that.

No Emily I'm not trying to tease you I'm saying the fact when next we see we are going to celebrate it together. Okay dear thanks for that, I can't wait for that day to come dear.

Calm down Emily, it's just a small celebration.

I know Henry, just that I can't wait for that day. I'm super excited about it,my love.

Okay, Emily, I have to go now.

All right, dear, take care of yourself, and thanks for the time.

Bye, I hang up.

Mummy, I think I need to change my phone.
" Why do you want to change it?
" Mum, I am now a big girl, I need a bigger phone.
"Okay Emily, don't worry I'll see to that, but till next year.
Yeh!!!!!
Mum, why next year
"Yes, my daughter till next year, so relax.
Mum, why?
That got me thinking, I had no choice but to wait for another year. Anyway, it was worth the wait.
I went straight to my bedroom to finish my work before going to bed.

Bright Sunny day
The sound of my phone woke me up, stretching my body, as I was weak. It was quite stressful for me last night.
When I checked my time, it was 7:30.
I stood up from the bed, to do the right thing I needed to do on time.
Thanks for the dinner, my love...
I can't express how happy I am for this big celebration just because of the promotion you promised me and you fulfilled it. I appreciate it. Thank you so much.
It's nothing Emily, you are my girlfriend so I have to take care of you and treat you as a queen.
I'm blushing, I said.
After the dinner party, he escorts me to the front of my house. We had a romantic dinner together. He gave me a peck and left.
I stepped into the house. I met my mom in the sitting room.
We need to talk, my dear.
Can I take a shower first, mum? She shakes her head and says okay. After that, I went to the bathroom.
I sit next to her and I calm my mind to get her attention. " Mum, hope your problem, why aren't you saying anything? I tried to read my mother's face, but I can't describe what she was thinking.
" Do you love me?
" Of course, I love you, Mum. What happened? What do you want to talk about?
" I want you to stop seeing Henry."
" What!!!!
Why should I stop seeing him? We are just friends. I'm sorry Mum I can't do that, it's impossible.
Emily, you are a kid you don't understand most people are out there saying trash about you and this guy you're walking with, as you know your dad is a minister, and I don't want anything to ruin his image.
Mum, I can't do that. I'm sorry. " You have to do that,I am your mother, " she said.
I did not believe what she said. I can't live without him, who am I supposed to love if not for Henry, I was shattered.
"Mum, it's not funny, " I laughed, but she was quite serious. My mum isn't joking. Her expression is so serious right now. No, you can't do this to me Mum. She left me alone in the living room and went to her bedroom.

Without me knowing my eyes were full of tears, I hope it's all a dream and when I wake up tomorrow everything will be back to normal, I said.
I felt someone rock my body. I jerked. My eyes opened then I remembered what happened last night. What my mother said was not a dream, I was back to reality, and I cried.
It's my life and I will make my own choice. I was crying, sitting down in front of the door, my feet were shaking, I put my head on my knees, I did not know how many hours had passed, I stood up and went to the bathroom to freshen up. I took a cold shower at the same time I was crying.
My phone was ringing, I looked at the screen and it was Henry. Yes, I need him now.
"Babe......
" Y...es, " I replied.
" Why are you sounding like this Emily?
I was crying, I could not talk.......
" Babe talk to me please".
" Henry, I can't talk..... Okay Emily I'm coming to your side, he said. Hearing that I shouted, "No"..... He was shocked. Why did you shout like that babe I'm sure something is wrong with you talking to me, he pleaded.
" Alright, I'll come to your place, I said. Quickly I opened my closet and searched for a top and jeans, I grabbed my phone running towards the gate. I went to Henry's house, not too far from my house.
I stopped in front of his house and I called out his name, "Henry."
Come inside Emily, I went inside, he offered me a cup of water.
but I refused. My eyes were red.

Chapter 7

"Emily, You don't seem so good. What happened?

My eyes were feeling and I couldn't hear anything, he sat next to me and grabbed my hand.

" Why is my life now so f****** hard I said, he looked at me and took a deep breath to organize his mind. I feel like I couldn't breathe normally, Closed my eyes trying to arrange my mind.

" What is wrong Emily, I'm all yours talk to me, " he said for the second time. After a while I explained everything to him with my eyes full of tears dropping. He could feel my pain, He came closer to me and hugged me. I felt so emotional I could not stop the tears from dropping. Why me!!!! I make a firm voice.

After some minutes I could sense Henry was quiet, he was hurt, He couldn't show it because he is a man but I could feel he was deeply hurt about what my mother said.

After everything I've gone through, should I start from the very first day I met Henry up to the time he finally accepts my love, and now that we too are in love with each other they want to separate us. We were in pain, the atmosphere was quiet.

****

Henry, what should we do about this, I said. because we are so confused that we don't know what to do and we can't live without each other.

" I'm so confused, Emily, " he said.

But Emily promises me no one will come in between us.

I promise you no one will come in between us and not even our parents, I assured him.

Then we make a plan not to talk to each other physically except on call or WhatsApp. Henry, you need to change my name on your phone, And I'll do the same. Wow, Emily that is a great idea, he said.

Since then we have been talking mostly online so my parents won't suspect that I'm still with the same guy she asked me to stay far away from. Everything was going smoothly without any problem or disturbance little did I know that they are still much to come.

I read day and night preparing for my school exams. We just have two terms left to pass out. Everybody we're running helter-skelter from one school to another looking for whom to assist their children.

We set a time to call each other so no one will get suspicious about our movement or our secret affairs. Unfortunately, Henry's mother found out about us being together, she shouted at Henry just the way my mother did to me. Henry told me about what happened between him and his mum hearing that again I was weakened. Now both parents want us to be apart, falling from one problem to another. We were totally confused, and we don't know the next steps to take anymore.

We love each other so much but our parents are against it.

" Destiny is not a matter of chance but choice, you can be whoever you want to be if you strive hard and believe in yourself, just be good to yourself and wish out for the things you want". Life is a matter of choice and not chance.

I didn't give up on our love, I kept on striving Hard, we didn't allow our parents to become an obstacle to our love story, we pushed further and aimed high.

They are indeed our parents, it is part of the role they often play and sometimes beyond it when their children get to a mature age.

But we aren't affected by that. is not that we are disobedient to them, just fighting for what gives us happiness. Our love is not our weakness rather it gives us more confidence and the ability to think and pursue our future. however, they are some love who after sex and lust of the flesh but ours was different, the fire of love burning in us gives us more confidence, and determination to pursue our dream, Focus, and clarity of goals to be pursued.

Our love story isn't an easy one, but still, we didn't give up. We refused to be separated.

"Life is a mystery, just like a beautiful flower, situations fluctuate at times. We go through life from infancy to old age with a mixture of experiences including joy and Sorrow, happiness and sadness, and triumph and tribulation. life is a race of the utilization of opportunities and privileges. Which is what we are doing.

I count my love as an opportunity that can't be retrieved if it gets lost due to our parents' wrong movement.

"Everything is fair in love"

Good morning dear.

It's Henry on the phone.

My phone light blinded me for a second. Oh lord, this light will not kill me!!!!

After a few seconds, my pupils started adjusting to the bright light.

" How are you, dear, hope you are well.

" I'm not fine Emily, he broke down. He started crying with all his might, knowing that Henry is unhappy and hurt even more. " I Can't Live Without You Emily, people think of me as a strong person but I was never a strong person. I am weak from inside. How could I be strong when so much pain was buried inside my heart and the pain was because of my parent's Disapproval of our relationship? They are troubling me a lot to leave you but I can't do that. Emily, I don't know what to do, I can stay without you.

" I could sense the sincerity in his voice. I tried to be strong. our whole world is about to crush down, I was shattered like a broken Mirror. I had to stay strong because of my upcoming examination.

" Henry, I'm using this medium to assure you that nothing will separate us, " I assured him, and he was happy about it. I wasn't aware that I was capable of enduring so much pain and that is what is killing me. tears had stopped coming out of his eyes.

I just want you to be happy Henry please for my sake, I said.

I couldn't stop thinking about our issues. Like my examination, I was facing hell at home. My mum wasn't easy on me at all, she frustrates me all the time just because I insist on keeping my relationship with Henry. Sometimes I sit alone crying, I didn't tell Henry about it, because if he hears about it, he might want to give up on our love.

I endure numerous insults from my parents and Henry's family to the extent that no one in the Henry family loves me except for his little brother. Both of them love me so much, that gave me more confidence. My mum asked someone to monitor my movements just to confirm if I'm still with Henry or not.

Chapter 8

All I desired was to live a happy life but our family is making it unbearable for us, so many times my parents will cease my phone and lock me inside for days, for me not to come in contact with Henry or hear from him. Henry is such an understanding person, he also faced a lot from his own family but yet we keep on allowing the fire of our love to burn in us.
I wasn't distracted at all nor did I allow my love for Henry to fade, I keep on trying, and soon things will become better.
Three months after
I was preparing for my examination. There are two weeks left before the commencement of our exam. I keep on reading for me to come out with flying colors.
My phone was ringing.
Wow, it was Henry. "Hi, my love !!!
How are you doing Emily, Hope you are studying hard my love, I want you to come out with flying colors.
" Sure dear, I'll make you my parents proud, " I said to him. Before I could say anything I heard a voice from the background, it was Henry's mother shouting at him.
"Henry didn't I tell you not to call this girl anymore, or have anything to do with her". I was speechless. I decided to end the call so as not to cause more problems for him, I was crying.
I know I shouldn't feel like that but I couldn't help it watching Henry being scolded because of me.
Is it a crime to fall in love? I asked myself, hitting my hand on my head. Why am I so unlucky I said, crying heavily. This pain and torture became unbearable for me, It reached a point I could not bear it anymore, every day I get the beating of my life all in the name of "love".
I decided to stop seeing Henry because I couldn't bear the pain of seeing him scolded by his family and hated by my own family. This is going beyond our expectations.
I didn't move away from him because I didn't love him, but I did that to make him happy, little did I know he can't be happy without me by himself, then we decided to all problems, hatred and scolding together, our love story wasn't an easy one.

A day to my examination!!!
Preparing my dress to go out on a date with Henry, somewhere far from our house. I put on my short skirt and top with my handbag, then I exited the room.
A few minutes later...
I was at the location, exactly where Henry said we should meet, it's one of our favorite hangouts which no one is aware of.
"Hi dear"
He hugged me and planted a kiss on my forehead. I was happy and blushing. "me and my blushing problem, I said.
"Henry, How are you doing?
" I'm fine babe and it's all because of you, he pulled my cheek laughing like a baby.
" Oh stop that Henry, You want me to stop blushing, isn't it? It's not a bad thing if you blush my darling wife, he said.
"Wife!!!!!

I was shocked.....
" Yes dear, because no one can take your place in my life, I love you much more than you can imagine. That is the reason why I endure so much pain, it's all because of the love I have for you. I don't want anyone else as my wife except for you Emily.
Hearing those words made my cheek turn red, I could not hide it anymore then I smiled at him holding his two hands lovingly. Thank you so much, Henry, for everything you've done so far, You stood by me whenever I needed someone to share my pains with, You never forsake me, I appreciate that, Thank you so much, Henry, I said.
" You don't need to thank me, Emily, I should be the one thanking you, my loving wife, " he said. we both smiled.....
Our day went so well, "I wish we could always stay happy like this without any interference," I said to myself. Hmmm...... (Sign of relief).
That reminds me, babe, Tomorrow is your exam, isn't it?
" Yes Tomorrow is my exam"
" Oh, I trust you are well prepared, my loving wife.
After the discussion, he prayed for me and wished me success in my examination.
Indeed I'm so lucky to have Henry by my side, he's a loving boyfriend, so caring and adorable.
After the meal, we decided to go home because of our parents before they'll start questioning our whereabouts.

The moment was so adorable.
We exited the restaurant and left. I got home around 5 p.m, I went straight to the bathroom to freshen up.
I clear my room and pack my books to where they belong. immediately I finish doing that, I gather all the materials I'll be needing tomorrow in the exam Hall.

A few hours later
Around 9 p.m.....
I received a text message from Henry, it was an admission letter.
Henry has been given admission to study his dream course "computer engineering". I was so happy for him but then I was sad as well.
Henry will be leaving for another city makes me sad. I'm addicted to being around him, how will I cope?
Immediately I called him then he went outside to pick up his call because of his mum. Truly I was happy for him but then I explained to him.
"Henry, how are we going to cope with being apart from each other? For a few minutes, there was silence between us.

"Hmmm... Emily I understand your points of view, it's true and I understand you but remember distance is not the barrier. believe in our love, and remember it's not a life journey but from some years and that does not mean I won't come home, my love.
Okay Henry I understand but promise me you always come home at least once a month and you always call me every day.
" I promise to do that, "baby girl"...... Okay dear, we both smile.

Don't stress yourself too much dear, Still have one week to spend with you before I leave. Moreover, tomorrow is your exam. Please don't allow that to affect your exam, okay?
Alright Henry I've heard you, We'll talk later take care of yourself, bye.
"Bye"
Talking to Henry makes me feel happy, I can't imagine how my life would be if Henry was not in my life, so grateful for having him as my future partner. I went to bed, and slept peacefully.

Chapter 9

Yawning as I was stretching my body.....
I feel like sleeping more, I said.
I checked my time, and whoa, it was 6am already. I jumped up instantly to do my chores, it took me 15 minutes to finish that stuff. After some hours, I exited my room, went to my parents, and they both prayed for me.
On my way, I passed through Henry's house.
"Stop"
I heard a small firm voice... I checked back to see who it was. It was Henry waiting to bid me farewell and wish me success. He came closer to me and gave me a sweet to eat, after that he kissed me. "I wish you success my love", he said.
Thanks so much, Henry, I have to be on my way now.
"Take care of yourself Emily I'll miss you"
Don't worry I'll be back before you know it, I said. I went on my own.

On getting to school, I saw so much preparation being done already, I went to my class, bowed my head, and prayed to God.
Not quite long after the invigilator came in, we started our exam.
All glory to God, my first paper was awesome. After my exam, I went home to prepare more for tomorrow's exam as well.
I picked up my call to dial Henry's number.
"Good afternoon my love.
" Good afternoon my baby girl.
How are you doing, I said.
I'm fine Emily, and what about you? How was today's exam?
It was good Henry, I said.
That my baby girl, I trust you.
That reminds me, your birthday is on the way, I can't wait to celebrate the third birthday with you, Emily.
Yes oh, Henry.

****

The exam went so well, a little bit tough, but all glory to God. I was done with my exam. All the students were after their results, most parents were bribing the teachers to assist their children.
"The ability to develop intelligence has nothing to do with your race, color, or background. As an individual, you are solely responsible for your actions.
Our classroom was like an athletic field where winners are the front runners, and others outran automatically become just part of the race. The choice of the position I intend to strive for, I need to acquire it. I put all my effort into my exam to get that position.
I create and devote extra time to studying difficult subjects. I make friends with the best students in different subjects to acquire more knowledge.

One month later

I got a message that our results had been released. I quickly grabbed my phone to check my result. What is wrong with this network? I was complaining about the network issue.
The weather is cool so why is the network fluctuating....
My mind was not settled, I developed cold feet, and I was scared. What will be the outcome of my results, I don't want failure. I am not ready to resit for any examination again, I keep praying for good news.
Finally, my results came out, with the help of my teacher. Yeh !!!!!
I shouted in joy, I can't believe what I'm seeing.
I came out with distinction in all my subjects, I was so happy and full of joy
I pick up my phone to share the good news with Henry.
"Hello, sweetheart.
" Good afternoon baby girl, how are you doing today?
Am good Henry.
Hey, why are you so happy today, he asked.
Wait, how do you know I am happy? Why won't I know, have you forgotten we are one already, we are attached.
Anyway, no problem about that, I said. But I have very big news for you.
Really, what is the big news Emily, don't keep me in suspense.
"You won't believe I came out with an overall distinction in all my subjects and also they give me the scholarship to study in any country of my choice, but have decided to use my scholarship here by studying in this country, so we won't fall apart.
"Wow that call for a big celebration, I am so proud of you Emily.
Alright dear, I have to end the call now. I want to share the good news with my parents, I'm sure they'll be happy to hear that.
" Okay baby see you later, bye.
I was so happy, dancing all about in the house, I could not hide my happiness.
"Hello, mummy...
How are you Emily, hope no problem.
No mum, just have good news to share with you.
" Really what is that my love....
Mum, my results are out. Wow, I am happy for you, hope you've checked it.
Mum, you won't believe I came out with distinction in all my papers. That's not all, I have been granted a scholarship to study in any country of my choice, as a medical student.
Mum is so happy...
Wow, Emily, I knew you'd make us proud one day, thank you so much for making us proud.
Yes, mum, I am so grateful to God and Henry, all thanks to him. "Why do you make use of your two ears Emily?
Mum, it's not like that, all this thing I achieved was because of Henry, who supported me and gave me confidence.
" Shut up Emily, okay don't worry I know what to do.
"Mum, what are you saying?
" Don't worry you'll find out on your birthday.
I was shocked. What is my mum going to do? I was totally confused.
****

A week to my birthday…

I went for my birthday photoshoot, I can't believe I'll be clocking 18 years old, finally, I am now an adult, I said to myself. That reminds me, this week will make it 4 years of being in a relationship with Henry.

Wow indeed am such a brave girl, for the past 4 years have been enduring so many pains all in the name of "love"

All the preparations were going on for the celebration. Do you know how most people these days say that they don't like celebrating their birthday? Well, I have always been a birthday girl. Each year I am more excited about my birthday than the last.

I like to be pampered and treated like a princess throughout. This year I felt that my 18th birthday would be the best since I have my boyfriend to share my happiness with.

Finally, on the big day, the clock struck 12 and the doorbell of our house rang! With my phone ringing at the same time.

I picked up my call to check who it was, it was an unknown number. I answered the call, and at the same time, I opened the door.

"Hello, birthday princess!!!!

The voice sounds so familiar, Henry!!!

I know it's you okay…. Lol, he said.

"Happy birthday to you

Happy birthday to you

Happy birthday, to you Emily

Happy birthday to you.

Hip hip hip…hooray.

I have a surprise for you, Emily.

"What is it? Check your doorstep and see for yourself. I was about to ask something else, then he hung up.

I opened the door, and to my greatest surprise, I saw a standing teddy bear wearing a gown with a sign of " I love you". A lot of gifts were beside the teddy bear. I was full of joy. The teddy bear alone is something I can't express. Have been dreaming of having a teddy bear from a loved one, and today my dream was fulfilled. The gifts look so adorable.

I picked up my phone to call him but then it was switched off. I know he did that intentionally so I won't be able to say thank you.

We both understand each other, and the chemistry between us is so strong.

Henry was the first person to wish me a happy birthday, but no sign of my parents wishing me a happy birthday. I tried not to feel bad about it, after which I answered numerous birthday wish phone calls. I went to bed.

I was woken up in the morning by my two siblings, William and Sophia. Asking me to get ready by after 12…..

I was confused with no idea what was going on. They told me mum and dad wanted me to come to a place. It took me a few hours to fathom what was going on.

Chapter 10

Exactly noon…I was done brushing my teeth. I took my bath and put on my birthday cloth, the ones Henry gave to me as a gift to wear on my birthday. "My siblings dressed me as a bride going for registry"

I took my handbag, and my uncle was sitting in his car, which had a lot of balloons tied to the car. I slipped in, I was confused, and I had no idea what was happening.

Uncle, where are we going? I asked, don't worry Emily, you'll get to know that yourself. It took us 20 minutes to get there.

On getting there I saw a very big hall, well decorated with balloons and flowers, ahead of me. I saw my name at the entrance.

"Happy birthday to my first daughter"

I was getting butterflies in my tummy.

Two of my friends came out to take me in, I stepped my foot into the hall, and I was amazed.

Everybody was shouting"happy birthday Emily"

Happy tears started flowing down my eyes. What a loving parent I have. My birthday cake was 6 steps, similar to a wedding cake.

I was filled with joy, a lot of people were there. The decoration was awesome, the party went so well.

People were giving me gifts and wishes, and the noise and all the songs were giving me more joy.

We danced, danced, and danced. Everybody was excited including me, the celebrant.

I lighted up my eyes, I saw Henry coming inside, I was surprised, how come he knows I am there?

Have forgotten that all my dad's members were invited.

I was happy seeing him, I went to meet him, and he gave me a flying kiss, I was blushing.

****

It was time to cut the cake….

Everything was going smoothly, the cake was cut and distributed to everybody. I could not spend time with Henry very well.

Most of my friends were introducing me to their parents. After a while, I was called to give a speech.

"Hummm…..I don't even know what to say but all I would say is a very big thank you to you all, I am grateful and I appreciate you all for celebrating this special day with me". People were clapping.

After that, my parents said they have one more gift to give me.

Wow mum, what is it?

It's your birthday gift, but mum all this celebration is enough already, why do you still want to take the trouble to give me another gift

"You won't understand Emily, you are our first fruit, we have to secure your future and provide all the necessary things you want.

Okay, mum. Am waiting for it, I said.

Everywhere was quiet, thinking about what the gift was all about.

Henry was smiling at me, assuring me everything will be fine. Soon after my mum came out with a white envelope, and she handed it over to me.

"Mum what is this…open it, Emily, it contains your birthday gift. I opened the white envelope to check what was inside. Immediately I dropped the envelope on the floor. I shouted mum, what is this, is this the gift you are talking about? " Mum this is a visa to the USA, my eyes were full of tears. People were shouting,whoa hey, congrats, and so on.
They all think I was happy seeing the visa, but Henry understood everything, he knows how deeply hurt I was. I looked at him, his eyes were full of tears, he rushed out and went home.
I had no choice but to control my emotions, because of the multitude, so my parents won't be disgraced.
Throughout the celebration I wasn't myself, I put on a fake smile so people won't notice my sad face.
On getting home I went to meet my parents. Mom, dad, why did you do this to me? I know your intention. You want me to go so the relationship between Henry and I would break off. Mum why did you choose to do this to me, you know I love Henry so much. If you had asked for my life, I would gladly give it to you instead you want to separate me from the love of my life, it's unfair mum.
She drew nearer to me, and slap me
Whether you like it or not Emily, you are going to the USA, tomorrow is your flight, so get ready.
I was heartbroken and short of words. I was crying heavily in my room.
Henry's call came in.
Hello……I was stammering.
"Emily please don't cry, I understand what you are going through, am also in pain but there's nothing I can do. They are your parents, they want the best for you, Emily.
Henry, am heartbroken, how do you want me to cope, staying away from you for seven years? It's not possible, I can't live without you, do you know the worst part of it? I am leaving tomorrow by 1 pm.
"Emily, don't think too much, but at least can we see tomorrow before your departure? Yes Henry, I also need to see you.
I wasn't able to sleep that day, I was busy crying throughout, till I became weak, I had no more power to cry, and I slept off while crying.
****

Next day
"Hello, Henry am there already. "Okay, I'm almost there.
I saw him from afar, and immediately I run to meet him, I hugged him, and my eyes were full of tears. We became so emotional, he was crying also.
" Emily calm down, everything will be fine, sit down, let's talk.
Henry, I can't live without you, it's not so easy to spend seven years without seeing you, I was crying.
He brought out his handkerchief and wiped my tears. "Emily is not easy for me as well, but we just have to be strong for one another, let's accept our date.
Henry…..(crying).......
I'll miss you so much……hmmm(crying). You'll always be in my heart, no one will ever take your place. I don't know if you'll wait for me, or if you'll be able to endure but please if you don't see me look for someone else, so I won't keep you waiting in vain. But I promise you I won't get

married to someone else, because I can't love anyone else except for you Henry, I said while crying heavily…hmmm...
Emily you've promised me, you won't marry anyone else, same here dear. Emily, I promise you today I won't get married to anyone else except for you. I promise to wait till you come back. He was crying as well. We were both in years, holding each other's hands. Immediately I got a call from my mum.
"Emily where are you, it's time already….
Hearing that I cried heavily, I held onto Henry's hand, I didn't feel like letting go….. "Emily it's time to go, no Henry I can't go, I can't, I was crying seriously.
I can't live without you Henry, do something I don't want to go, please.
He hugged me, kissed me for the last time and free his hands from mine, and left. I fell on my knees crying….. a day I can't forget.
Henry, don't go please, I shouted….
Henry, please don't go, I can't live without you, I was crying bitterly.
I stood up and went home to pick up my belongings. We were at the airport.
On getting there, we did all the necessary things. I didn't bother to hug my parents, I was deeply hurt, so I went up to the plane.
They both bid me farewell but I ignored them. On my way to the plane, I was crying. I looked back for the last time, but I didn't see Henry. I cried. It hurts so much to be separated from the person you love the most.

Chapter 11

A few hours later…

I didn't realize the plane has landed until a young lady touched me. I was lost in thought, remembering every moment I spent with Henry.

I was in the USA already

My uncle came to pick me up, on getting home, I searched for my handbag to pick up my phone, to give Henry a call but it wasn't there, then I remembered my bag was with my mum. She took my phone.

Why mum!!!!!

I shouted, now I have no hope of communicating with him, nor did I save his phone number offhand, I cried again.

****

Time flew very fast

I was in my fifth year, but still I couldn't get in touch with Henry. " I heard the news that he has relocated to another place.

Every day I miss him so much, sometimes I stare at his photo, and sometimes I cry, but yet I didn't give up. Instead I put more effort into my education to finish on time.

A day without Henry was like a thousand days before me.

I missed him so much, my love for him grew stronger.

Sometimes I get lost in thought, thinking about him….each time I remember him I always cry….. indeed I missed him so much.

He was my confidant, my adviser, my happiness, and my mentor……

I had to face everything all alone, I missed him so much. I wished he was here with me.

Two years later

Congratulations, I was greeting one of my friends, and at last, we made it.

Yes oh Emily, we made it.

At last, I fulfilled my dream of becoming a surgeon (a medical doctor).

It wasn't easy but we stick to it and we made it at last. Then I remember, when I got admission to school, I celebrated it with Henry, and when I passed out, we both celebrated it but now he isn't here to celebrate it with me, thinking about that I cried. I give thanks to God I made it. Finally I am going back to my city to be with Henry once again. I could not express how happy I was. Thinking about the fact that I am going back home to see Henry, makes my day great. I gather my stuff, certificate, my clothes, everything I have, preparing to leave the following day. That night was the longest night I had, I was happily staring at the time, so as not to miss my flight.

Yeah!!!!! The weather looks so cool, this place is just the same as when I left seven years ago. Wow, I missed my country so muy, especially Henry, I can't wait to see him and kiss him, I said. The breeze was blowing so cool, finally I am back once again.

My dad was at the airport waiting for me, seeing him I run to him, I gave him a tight hug, my eyes were full of tears.

"Dad I missed you so much, I cried…

" Emily I missed you so much also, I am sorry for causing you so much pain.
Let's go home dad it's getting late, throughout the moment I was in the car I was daydreaming about Henry, how we first met, and our love story began. It's so lovely to be back at home.
On getting home I saw my family waiting for me at the gate, my siblings rushed to hug me, and I was happy to see them. After so many years, I was excited. My mum was there waiting for me to hug her, but I went inside my room.
Stepping my foot into the room, remind me of some memories, WOW I touched my bed still the same as it was. Everything was adorable.
Not quite long, my mother came inside.
"Emily I know you are mad at me, for what I did seven years ago, I did that for you Emily please don't be mad at me. No mum you didn't do that for me you did that for your selfish reason but now I'm back again.
Emily, please forgive me, my child, I couldn't bear it. I went up to her and hugged her. I remember everything she has done so far. shed my mother I can't hurt her feelings, she hugged and cried.
Do you know how much I missed you Emily, each time I think about you but I don't want to become your weakness, am sorry my child?
Mum no problem, have forgiven you already.
My siblings were with me, and they all wanted me to gist them all about the USA. Indeed it was a great night for the family. They were happy to hear many things about the USA, especially my junior sister, Sophia.
We all went to bed.
****
Yeh!!!!!
Stretching my body, due to the journey, I was weak.
I freshen up, I went to Henry's house
On getting there I saw his mum.
"Good afternoon mum"
Good afternoon, please who are you?
Ma, this is Emily.
"Emily, Emily is that you, wow you've turned into a full grown-up girl, how is study, when did you arrive?
Ma It was yesterday, "okay.
Mum, what about Henry? "Henry is not around; he left the house almost three years ago.
But why did Henry leave the house and go? It's all my fault, Emily, I went against his relationship with you, after your departure. A few years later he left home one morning and till now we haven't seen him.
Aghh!!!! I shouted.
Where could he have gone, I said.
"Ok ma, I am going home, alright dear take care of yourself. lastly please can you forgive me for going against your relationship, you were too young then that was why I didn't approve of it.
No mum, I am not angry, goodbye ma.
"Bye dear"

I was so worried about where on earth will I look for Henry and go, I had no clue or his contact. I was damn worried.

Emily, yes mum do you remember your birthday is on Friday?
Yes, I remember, so how do you want to celebrate it? Mom I don't know, just make everything okay.
Alright, dear.
****
Still, in search of Henry, where are you Henry I said, crying....
Am back now but you are not here, this wasn't the promise we made to each other. Where are you?
Many days passed by with no traces of him, I was scared I didn't know what to do. I keep my hope alive.

Chapter 12

Fantastic it's my 25th birthday, so many calls, gifts.......I was happy but not full of happiness, Henry is not here with me.

Henry, where are you? Today is my birthday, I'm sure you remember, so why aren't you here, I said to myself with my two eyes closed. I was crying......

"Happy birthday Emily"

I was shocked, I opened my eyes. this voice looks familiar, I looked back to see who it was.

I shouted with my might....

Henry is that you....

Yes Emily it's me

Our eyes were full of tears, tears of joy.

I hugged him tightly as if I wasn't letting go of something. Where did you go to Henry, I kept questioning him.

Have looked everywhere for you, even mum said she does not know your whereabouts.

Why did you leave without telling anyone? I was breathing heavily.

Calm down Emily, today is your day relax, okay Henry have heard you.

That was a double joy indeed, after seven good years..... Henry was so happy, he hugged me, again and again, we were happy.....that was the most memorable birthday I have ever had.

****

Henry, let's go to your mum, she's worried about you, you shouldn't be angry at her, she is just fulfilling the role of a mother to you.

"Emily, I don't want to go there.

Okay dear, but for my sake let's go.

Alright, my love.

We went to his mum's house and on getting there we saw her crying.

Mum, why are you crying? I said.

*You won't understand my daughter. I missed my son so much, if I could see him, I will apologize for everything I have done to him.

Mum Henry is here, I said.

Instantly she jumped up, where is he?

Henry POV

Mom, I am here, Henry's mum was happy to see her son, she apologized for everything she did.

After that, she joined my hands with Henry and blessed us. I was happy.

"I would like you to be my son's wife, she said.

Hearing this Henry hugged his mother, and we were happy.

****

Henry, your mum has given her consent, what about my parents, I said.

" Don't Emily, everything will be good, if truly we are not meant to be we wouldn't have seen each other today. By the grace of God, your parents will accept our love story.

We went back to the birthday party.

My mum was giving a speech....

"Emily, I have a gift to give you for this birthday party.

What is it this time around? I was scared and hoped is not be another visa to spend 7 years again in another country. My heart was beating very fast……
She proceeds.
Emily, I want to give you a special gift that you'll remember for the rest of your life.
She brought out a board covered with a cloth.
"What is this, " I said.
" Open it, my daughter.
My hand was shaking, I was frightened. What could this be?
I removed the cloth, and look, it has handwriting written on it.
Written……" will you marry Henry"
Seeing that I fell to my knees, shouting "at last" tears were dropping out of my eyes, like a flowing river. Henry came to me, knee down, and held my hand, will you marry me in front of everybody?
People were shouting for joy. say, yes!!!!!!
"Yes, I said.
My parents were happy…..
Henry lift me, shouting this is my bride-to-be.
We went to my parents, knelt before them and they both prayed for us.

Day went by, months passed
Preparing for our wedding. …..
Glory be to God the day came to pass and it was a blissful day for both me and my husband (Henry).
A day I can't forget, it was a dream coming true. We took a family portrait of both parents. It was a great day for us.
Indeed we are destined to be together, I said.
We went through a lot but still, we didn't give up, we keep on striving hard, hoping someday things we'll be better, and here it comes. After our marriage, we live happily and today am, happily married with four children.

"My home,

A home of love, where peace reigns,

A home where you always want to be,

Where everybody is somebody.

Where love is expressed and shared,

My home, my heart, a sweet, lovely, and peaceful home.

Thank God, I have a home"

Conclusion

The love between two people poses a challenge, life is a mystery. Don't give up on your love story because of a little issue or problem, indeed one's success in life depends on how we organize it. This world is full of a mixture of experiences including joy and sorrow, happiness and sadness. Whatever challenges you are encountering other people are going through similar or even worse situations. Stay focused, be optimistic, and consider it solved. Life is so beautiful, yet so fragile.

"Keep your love alive"

DEDICATION

To my darling husband, Kingston,
My joy giver,
My confidant,
My advisor,
My happiness.
Thanks for always being there for me.

www.ingramcontent.com/pod-product-compliance
Lightning Source LLC
LaVergne TN
LVHW041303150826
845673LV00008B/2710

* 9 7 9 8 3 6 4 6 0 1 3 1 5 *